Create in Me A Clean Heart

Blessings!

Sarah Christopher

Psalm 1.

Create in Me
A Clean Heart

Ten Minutes a Day
in the Penitential Psalms

SARAH CHRISTMYER

www.ComeIntotheWord.com

Cover by Cynthia Oswald.
Photo by Sarah Christmyer. Statue of Jesus and Peter, "Feed My Sheep," Church of the Primacy of Peter, Tabgha, Israel.
Interior design by Stella Ziegler

ISBN-10: 1523494417
ISBN-13: 978-1523494415

Let each one, therefore, who recites the Psalms have a sure hope that through them God will speedily give ear to those who are in need. For if a man be in trouble when he says them, great comfort will he find in them; if he be tempted or persecuted, he will find himself abler to stand the test and will experience the protection of the Lord. [...] If he have sinned, when he uses them he will repent; if he have not sinned, he will find himself rejoicing that he is stretching out towards the things that are before [Phil 3:16] and, so wrestling, in the power of the Psalms he will prevail.

—St. Athanasius

Contents

Introduction

$\mathscr{E}$very year, Lent holds out the opportunity for a spiritual "cleanse"—a chance to open our hearts and allow the Holy Spirit to shine a light into dark corners, expose sin and pain, and bring it out for healing.

One time-honored custom that harnesses the power of God's word to read our hearts this way is praying the seven Penitential Psalms. All psalms help us express emotion and turn our hearts to God, but these in particular help us recognize our sin, offer up our sorrow, and ask for God's forgiveness. From the earliest days of the Church, Christians recited Psalm 51 (the Miserere) every morning. By at least the fifth century, four Penitential Psalms were recognized by St. Augustine. They were so meaningful to him that at the end of his life, he posted them by his bed in large print and recited them daily for the ten days leading up to his death. By the 6th century AD, Cassiodorus named seven "Penitential Psalms" or "Psalms of Confession" in his commentary. These[1] are the psalms we pray today at times of repentance and particularly during Lent:

---

[1] Protestant and modern Catholic translations of the Bible use the numbering given here, which is based on the Hebrew text of the Psalms. Eastern Orthodox Bibles and the Douay-Rheims version use a different numbering based on the Greek (Septuagint) text: Psalms 6, 31, 37, 50, 101, 129, and 142. The alternate numbering will often appear in brackets, for example: "Psalm 32[31]."

Psalm 6 – Prayer in distress and illness

Psalm 32 – Prayer for forgiveness of sin

Psalm 38 – Confession of sin and prayer for help

Psalm 51 – (*Miserere*) Prayer for God's mercy

Psalm 102 – Prayer in distress and affliction

Psalm 130 – (*De profundis*) Prayer from the depths; a soul waiting for God

Psalm 143 – Prayer of supplication, for deliverance

There is no one single way to pray the Penitential Psalms. **One traditional method** during Lent is to read all seven psalms together, possibly beginning and ending with a brief antiphon and separating each with a *Glory Be*. The antiphon might be like the one used in this book:

"Listen to me, O God, and show me mercy; for I am a sinner before you."

Another common practice is to pray a single psalm each day (which you may frame by an antiphon and a *Glory Be*), focusing on a different one each day or week.

A third, more contemplative method is the main subject of this book. It involves meditating on one psalm a week, 10 – 15 minutes a day for five days, with the goal of hearing God speak into your heart. It is not an intellectual study—it is a slow and careful listening for God's voice that can be very helpful in this penitential season.

[The chapter for the first week of Lent explains how to combine five days into three if you begin Ash Wednesday with the official start of Lent, instead of on Monday.]

—Monday: Prepare your heart

The first day, you will read a reflection that introduces the psalm before praying the psalm simply, out loud. You may choose to read the psalm from your own Bible, but the text is also included at the start of the chapter. As the week goes on you may find it helpful to mark up that copy: to underline key words, highlight things that stand out to you, note parallels and patterns, and so on.

—Tuesday – Friday: Prayerful reading

Days 2-5 involve 10 minutes a day of prayerful meditation on the psalm, going a little bit deeper each day in prayer. The steps are based on a time-tested method of reading Scripture so it becomes a prayerful conversation with the Lord: *lectio divina*—"spiritual reading," or, literally, "divine reading."

The process of *lectio divina* is simple: you read; you prayerfully think about what you read; you listen to it speak to your heart and respond to God; and you rest in his presence. Each step of the way, you are guided so that your meditation is infused with prayer. You can spend 10-15 minutes a day, or you can spend longer—it's up to you. If you are not familiar with *lectio divina*, there is a brief guide on page 7.

The value of repetition and journaling

Over the course of each week, you will read each Penitential Psalm many times over. It may seem pointless at first, to read and re-read the same words. Yet it is precisely in the repetition—even if it seems monotonous at first—that the richness comes.

You will also be given space to write down your observations and the fruits of your meditation and prayer as you go through the stages of praying each psalm. Writing is an excellent way to take the Word in deeper and remember what the Spirit brings to your mind. The more you allow the Word to penetrate your heart, the more you allow it to work *in* you—the more it will transform your life.

Ultimately, the word of God is not a book but a person who loves you and longs to connect with you on an intimate spiritual level. Take the opportunity Lent provides to offer up just 1% of your waking hours to get to know God:

Take 10-15 minutes a day … get away from it all … open your heart … and listen for his voice.

As you join me and Come into the Word this Lent—may you discover the living Word of God within the written words of the Penitential Psalms. And may they lead you to his arms of merciful love.

For the glory of God,
Sarah Christmyer
February 2016
Philadelphia

I am happy to answer any questions you have regarding this Lenten journal. Please email me: sarah@comeintotheword.com.

How to pray with Scripture: a brief guide to *lectio divina*

There is one particular way of listening to what the Lord wishes to tell us in his word and of letting ourselves be transformed by the Spirit. It is what we call lectio divina.

—Pope Francis, (Evangelii Gaudium, 152)

Growing up in a Protestant family, I was used to settling down with my Bible and reading until I heard the Lord speaking to me. Little did I know, I was unconsciously following a very ancient practice of praying with Scripture. In the 11th century, a monk named Guigo the Carthusian described it as four rungs of a ladder that leads from earth to heaven: Reading, meditating, praying, and contemplating. The first step, reading (in Latin: *lectio*), gives the practice its name: *lectio divina*, divine (or spiritual) reading. When these steps are followed, the reader is drawn into a prayerful conversation with the Lord.

The "four Rs" of *lectio divina*

If you're new to *lectio divina*, it might be useful to think of these steps as four "Rs" that lead you into an intimate conversation with God: **Read — Reflect — Respond — Rest**.

It's not complicated.

You simply read and think carefully about what you read ... listen for what God might be saying to you ... talk to him about what you hear ... and rest in his presence.

Here's how it's done:

1. Pray before you begin

> *Prayer should accompany the reading of Sacred Scripture, so that God and man may talk together; for "we speak to Him when we pray; we hear Him when we read the divine saying."*
>
> —*Pope Paul VI (Dei Verbum, 25)*

Open your heart and ask the Lord to speak. Prepare to listen. If you're distracted, ask for help. Ask God to help you hear and focus. Ask Jesus, the living Word, to speak to you. Ask the Holy Spirit to come and fill you. Ask Mary, Mother of the Word, to pray for you. She more than any other human knows what it is like to receive God's word and ponder it in such a way that it bears fruit.

2. Read

> *[Lectio Divina] consists of reading God's word in a moment of prayer and allowing it to enlighten and renew us.*
>
> —*Pope Francis (Evangelii Gaudium, 152)*

Choose a small passage of Scripture. Read it slowly three to five times or more until you are very familiar with what is being said.

Explore the passage you are reading. Notice details, gather facts. Look for the Who, What, When, and Where. Pay attention to patterns, to things that are repeated. It is most helpful to keep a journal to write down the things that you notice, or to underline and make notes on the text itself. The text of the Penitential Psalms is provided in this journal for that purpose.

3. Reflect

In the presence of God, during a recollected reading of the text, it is good to ask, for example: "Lord, what does this text say to me?

—*Pope Francis (Evangelii Gaudium, 153)*

Turn from thinking and observing to meditating. In Hebrew, to meditate is to "chew" on the Word of God, getting out every last bit of flavor.

How do you "chew" on the Word? Think. Ponder. Ask things like How? Why? What does it mean?

As you reflect, ask God to speak through his Word to you. Set aside things you don't understand for another day. Listen for God's still, small voice within your heart.

4. Respond

…no one is more patient than God our Father…. He simply asks that we sincerely look at our life and present ourselves honestly before him, and that we be willing to continue to grow, asking from him what we ourselves cannot as yet achieve.

—*Pope Francis (Evangelii Gaudium, 153)*

Talk to the Lord about what you hear. If you hear a question – answer. If you have a question – ask. If you feel grateful – give thanks. There's not one right way to talk to God. Here are some biblical examples:

- Mary pondered what she heard in her heart (Luke 2:19).

- Abraham argued with God (Genesis 18:16-33).

- Jacob wrestled with him (Genesis 32:22-32).

- The father of the son possessed by demons said: "Lord I believe; help my unbelief!" (Mark 9:23-24).

- What is in your heart? Talk to God about it. Stay with Him and expect an answer. As you pray, listen. And resolve to act on what you hear.

5. Rest in God's presence and love.

Lectio Divina is truly 'capable of opening up to the faithful the treasures of God's word, but also of bringing about an encounter with Christ, the living word of God.'

—*Pope Benedict XVI (Verbum Domini, 87)*

Sometimes this step of resting is called "contemplation." It is less something you do than it is the result of what you have been doing. Your mind is lifted to God, and you experience His presence with joy and peace.

For more information about *lectio divina* and free downloads, including a one-page handout with a suggested journal format, go to the **"Take it to"** tab on my website, www.comeintotheword.com.

Take it with you:
Planting the Word in your heart

I have laid up thy word in my heart,
that I might not sin against thee.

—*Psalm 119:11*

*W*hen God speaks to you, resolve to plant his Word in your heart where it can take root and transform you from the inside out.

You will be doing this as you ponder the Penitential Psalms. Another way is to memorize Scripture. It's easier than you might think. Choose a verse that spoke to you from the Penitential Psalms, copy it onto a small card and carry it with you during the day. Take out the card whenever you have a few moments and repeat it to yourself (the reference too, so you know where to find it in your Bible!) until you know it. Or put a reminder on your smart phone. Set your alarm for noon and recite the verse before praying the Angelus. Do whatever will help you remember.

When you're done with one verse, post it over your desk or above your kitchen sink or on the dashboard of your car—somewhere you will see it and remember to review it. Meanwhile, start learning a new verse. Over time, you'll find that the Holy Spirit brings them to mind when you need them.

Week One:
Psalm 6

Prayer in distress and illness

Psalm 6

To the choirmaster: with stringed instruments; according to The Sheminith[2].
A Psalm of David.

1   O Lord, rebuke me not in thy anger,
       nor chasten me in thy wrath.
2   Be gracious to me, O Lord, for I am languishing;
       O Lord, heal me, for my bones are troubled.
3   My soul also is sorely troubled.
       But thou, O Lord—how long?
4   Turn, O Lord, save my life;
       deliver me for the sake of thy steadfast love.
5   For in death there is no remembrance of thee;

---

2   Exact meaning unknown. Probably a musical or liturgical term.

in Sheol who can give thee praise?

6   I am weary with my moaning;

> every night I flood my bed with tears;
> I drench my couch with my weeping.

7   My eye wastes away because of grief,

> it grows weak because of all my foes.

8   Depart from me, all you workers of evil;

> for the Lord has heard the sound of my weeping.

9   The Lord has heard my supplication;

> the Lord accepts my prayer.

10 All my enemies shall be ashamed and sorely troubled;

> they shall turn back, and be put to shame in a moment.

If you begin this week on Ash Wednesday instead of
on Monday: do Monday and Tuesday together; then
Wednesday by itself; then combine Thursday and Friday.

MONDAY
Prepare Your Heart

† Find a quiet place where you can read and pray without distraction.

† Close your eyes and place yourself in God's presence.

† Read the following:

Reflection

Psalm 6 draws us into the heart of a man who is suffering. It is a "prayer for recovery from grave illness" but it hints of other kinds of suffering, too: that of a "sorely troubled" soul, and the kind that comes from "foes" and "workers of evil." How are we to read this – particularly today, the first week of Lent, when it calls to us as a Penitential Psalm?

Old Testament Israel saw a connection between sin and evil and physical illness. Jesus draws on this when he heals people who are sick, to illustrate the far deeper healing of forgiveness that he brings with his kingdom. We can pray this psalm in physical illness or when we're under attack from the outside because God is our help and our healer in all sorts of situations. But it applies equally to the soul-sick anguish caused by sin. If it were not for sin, those other troubles would not be present. They are a sign and often a cause of separation from God.

There is a beautiful paradox at the start of this psalm. "O Lord, rebuke me not in your anger…. But thou, O Lord, how long?"

God "punishes" sin by allowing its consequences to overtake us. This is the "tough love" of a Father who longs for his children to be whole and full of life. He stands ready always with open arms, ready to forgive for the sake of his "steadfast love" (vs. 4). The word in Hebrew is *hesed*, "loving kindness." It is the deep, faithful, merciful love of a true father. Take to him the ills of your soul. He will hear the sound of your weeping and accept your prayer. And your enemies – whether they be real or imagined, physical or spiritual – shall be "ashamed and sorely troubled" while you are set free.

> *I have seen his ways, but I will heal him; I will lead him*
> *and requite him with comfort … Peace, peace, to the far*
> *and to the near, says the Lord; and I will heal him.*

> —Isaiah 57:18-19

† Pray Psalm 6 out loud, as follows.

Listen to me, O God, and show me mercy; for I am a sinner before you.

Prayerfully read the psalm.

Glory Be…

✐ TUESDAY ✐
Read

† Find a quiet place where you can read and pray without distraction.

† Close your eyes and place yourself in God's presence.

† Pray:

Lord, inspire me to read your Scriptures and to meditate upon them day and night…. I know that understanding and good intentions are worthless, unless rooted in your graceful love. I ask that the words of Scripture may also be not just signs on a page, but channels of grace into my heart.

——Origen of Alexandria

† Read Psalm 6 all the way through several times.

What stands out to you in this psalm? Are there any words or phrases that catch your eye? What do you notice about them? Record your thoughts here or in a journal if desired:

_____

_____

_____

_____

_____

_____

_____

---

† Pray Psalm 6 out loud, as follows.

Listen to me, O God, and show me mercy; for I am a sinner before you.

Prayerfully read the psalm.

Glory Be…

TAKE IT WITH YOU:

Copy the part of Psalm 6 that spoke most to you onto a small card or make a note on your smart phone. Carry it with you and meditate on it throughout the week. Repeat it until you know it by heart.

WEDNESDAY
Reflect

† Find a quiet place where you can read and pray without distraction.

† Close your eyes and place yourself in God's presence.

† Pray:

Lord, inspire me to read your Scriptures and to meditate upon them day and night…. I know that understanding and good intentions are worthless, unless rooted in your graceful love. I ask that the words of Scripture may also be not just signs on a page, but channels of grace into my heart.

—*Origen of Alexandria*

Reflect on Psalm 6, recalling your previous observations.

Continue to read, lingering where your heart draws you. What do you hear God saying to you, personally? Write down what comes to mind:

_____

_____

_____

_____

_____

_____

_____

_____

_____

_____

_____

_____

_____

_____

_____

_____

_____

_____

_____

_____

_____

† Pray Psalm 6 out loud, as follows.

Listen to me, O God, and show me mercy; for I am a sinner before you.

Prayerfully read the psalm.

Glory Be…

THURSDAY

Respond

† Find a quiet place where you can read and pray without distraction.

† Close your eyes and place yourself in God's presence.

† Pray:

Lord, inspire me to read your Scriptures and to meditate upon them day and night.... I know that understanding and good intentions are worthless, unless rooted in your graceful love. I ask that the words of Scripture may also be not just signs on a page, but channels of grace into my heart.

—Origen of Alexandria

† Read Psalm 6 and recall what you have been hearing God say to your heart.

What is your response? Talk to him about it. Are you burdened by the consequences of sin in your life? Has God called to your mind a particular sin that you should take to Confession? Does the Psalm move you to gratefulness, that you should thank God? Tell him what is in your heart:

_____

_____

_____

_____

_____

_____

_____

_____

_____

_____

_____

_____

_____

_____

_____

_____

_____

† Pray Psalm 6 out loud, as follows.

Listen to me, O God, and show me mercy; for I am a sinner before you.

Prayerfully read the psalm.

Glory Be…

✧ FRIDAY ✧
Rest

† Find a quiet place where you can read and pray without distraction.

† Close your eyes and place yourself in God's presence. Pray Psalm 6 out loud, as follows.

Listen to me, O God, and show me mercy; for I am a sinner before you.

Prayerfully read the psalm.

Glory Be…

Fix your gaze upon God and rest in his merciful love. Allow yourself to be quiet in his presence. Rest as though you are lying in his arms. Let him fill you with comfort and peace.

Our Father…

I will restore health to you,
and your wounds I will heal,
says the Lord.

—*Jeremiah 30:17*

Week Two
Psalm 32 (31)

Prayer for forgiveness of sin

Psalm 32

A Psalm of David. A Maskil.[1]

1   Blessed is he whose transgression is forgiven,
    whose sin is covered.

2   Blessed is the man to whom the Lord imputes no iniquity,
    and in whose spirit there is no deceit.

3   When I declared not my sin, my body wasted away
    through my groaning all day long.

4   For day and night thy hand was heavy upon me;
    my strength was dried up as by the heat of summer. [Selah]

5   I acknowledged my sin to thee,
    and I did not hide my iniquity;

---

1   Exact meaning unknown. Probably a musical or liturgical term.

I said, "I will confess my transgressions to the Lord";

    then thou didst forgive the guilt of my sin. [Selah]

6   Therefore let every one who is godly

    offer prayer to thee;

    at a time of distress, in the rush of great waters,

    they shall not reach him.

7   Thou art a hiding place for me,

    thou preservest me from trouble;

    thou dost encompass me with deliverance. [Selah]

8   I will instruct you and teach you the way you should go;

    I will counsel you with my eye upon you.

9   Be not like a horse or a mule, without understanding,

    which must be curbed with bit and bridle,

    else it will not keep with you.

10 Many are the pangs of the wicked;

    but steadfast love surrounds him who trusts in the Lord.

11 Be glad in the Lord, and rejoice, O righteous,

    and shout for joy, all you upright in heart!

MONDAY
Prepare Your Heart

† Find a quiet place where you can read and pray without distraction.

† Close your eyes and place yourself in God's presence.

† Read the following:

Reflection

When I set out to read the Penitential Psalms, I expect them to draw me into dust and ashes, into mourning for my sins. What a surprise to read Psalm 32, and find myself lifted into joy!

> *"Blessed is he whose transgression is*
> *forgiven, whose sin is covered" (vs. 1)*
>
> *"At a time of distress, in the rush of great*
> *waters, they shall not reach him" (vs. 6)*
>
> *"Be glad in The Lord, shout for joy, all*
> *you upright in heart!" (vs. 11)*

This psalm of David encourages us to declare our sin, to confess it to God, to throw ourselves into his arms not for judgment but for deliverance. It's not the only psalm to do this, but I love the way it teaches us to pray in the process.

When you read Psalm 32 this week, notice the way the audience shifts (especially in the RSV-CE version quoted above): it is directed to you at the start; then as the psalmist gives an example from his own experience, he starts to speak to God. He goes back to you, then back to God again, until at the end he draws you into a mutual shout of praise. And the best part? In verses 8-9, God breaks in and speaks to you, himself.

This is *lectio divina* in action, long before it was ever called that. The word proclaimed or READ at the beginning is meditated on, drawn into the heart of the one praying and allowed to speak to his life experience. The psalmist REFLECTS on this; he RESPONDS to God; and the prayer becomes a conversation. It ends in the "REST" of God's enveloping love and goes forth in the action of a call to others to rejoice.

Lectio divina: Read … Reflect … Respond … Rest.

Allow Psalm 32 to feed you this week, to draw you into God's presence. And may it color your penitence with the hope of joy to come.

† Pray Psalm 32 out loud, as follows.

Listen to me, O God, and show me mercy; for I am a sinner before you.
Prayerfully read the psalm.
Glory Be…

TUESDAY
READ

† Find a quiet place where you can read and pray without distraction.

† Close your eyes and place yourself in God's presence.

† Pray:

Lord, inspire me to read your Scriptures and to meditate upon them day and night.... I know that understanding and good intentions are worthless, unless rooted in your graceful love. I ask that the words of Scripture may also be not just signs on a page, but channels of grace into my heart.

—*Origen of Alexandria*

† Read Psalm 32 all the way through several times.

What stands out to you in this psalm? Are there any words or phrases that catch your eye? What do you notice about them? Record your thoughts here or in a journal if desired:

_____

_____

_____

_____

_____

_____

_____

_____

_____

_____

_____

_____

_____

_____

_____

_____

_____

† Pray Psalm 32 out loud, as follows.

Listen to me, O God, and show me mercy; for I am a sinner before you.

Prayerfully read the psalm.

Glory Be…

TAKE IT WITH YOU

Copy the part of Psalm 32 that spoke most to you onto a small card or make a note on your smart phone. Carry it with you and meditate on it throughout the week. Repeat it until you know it by heart.

WEDNESDAY
REFLECT

† Find a quiet place where you can read and pray without distraction.

† Close your eyes and place yourself in God's presence.

† Pray:

Lord, inspire me to read your Scriptures and to meditate upon them day and night…. I know that understanding and good intentions are worthless, unless rooted in your graceful love. I ask that the words of Scripture may also be not just signs on a page, but channels of grace into my heart.

—*Origen of Alexandria*

Reflect on Psalm 32, recalling your previous observations.

Continue to read, lingering where your heart draws you. What do you hear God saying to you, personally? Write down what comes to mind:

_____

_____

_____

_____

_____

_____

† Pray Psalm 32 out loud, as follows.

Listen to me, O God, and show me mercy; for I am a sinner before you.

Prayerfully read the psalm.

Glory Be…

THURSDAY

RESPOND

† Find a quiet place where you can read and pray without distraction.

† Close your eyes and place yourself in God's presence.

† Pray:

Lord, inspire me to read your Scriptures and to meditate upon them day and night.... I know that understanding and good intentions are worthless, unless rooted in your graceful love. I ask that the words of Scripture may also be not just signs on a page, but channels of grace into my heart.

—Origen of Alexandria

† Read Psalm 32 and recall what you have been hearing God say to your heart.

What is your response? Talk to him about it. Are you burdened by the consequences of sin in your life? Has God called to your mind a particular sin that you should take to Confession? Does the Psalm move you to gratefulness, that you should thank God? Tell him what is in your heart:

_____

_____

_____

_____

_____

† Pray Psalm 32 out loud, as follows.

Listen to me, O God, and show me mercy; for I am a sinner before you.

Prayerfully read the psalm.

Glory Be…

FRIDAY
REST

† Find a quiet place where you can read and pray without distraction.

† Close your eyes and place yourself in God's presence. Pray Psalm 32 out loud, as follows.

Listen to me, O God, and show me mercy; for I am a sinner before you.

Prayerfully read the psalm.

Glory Be…

🐚 **Fix your gaze upon God and rest in his merciful love.** Allow yourself to be quiet in his presence. Rest as though you are lying in his arms. Let him fill you with comfort and peace.

Our Father…

Many are the pangs of the wicked;
but steadfast love surrounds him who trusts in the Lord.

—Psalm 32:10

Week Three
Psalm 38 [37]

Confession of sin and prayer for help

Psalm 38

A Psalm of David, for the memorial offering.

1   O Lord, rebuke me not in thy anger,
     nor chasten me in thy wrath!

2   For thy arrows have sunk into me,
     and thy hand has come down on me.

3   There is no soundness in my flesh
     because of thy indignation;
     there is no health in my bones
     because of my sin.

4   For my iniquities have gone over my head;
     they weigh like a burden too heavy for me.

5   My wounds grow foul and fester

because of my foolishness,

6 I am utterly bowed down and prostrate;
     all the day I go about mourning.

7 For my loins are filled with burning,
     and there is no soundness in my flesh.

8 I am utterly spent and crushed;
     I groan because of the tumult of my heart.

9 Lord, all my longing is known to thee,
     my sighing is not hidden from thee.

10 My heart throbs, my strength fails me;
     and the light of my eyes—it also has gone from me.

11 My friends and companions stand aloof from my plague,
     and my kinsmen stand afar off.

12 Those who seek my life lay their snares,
     those who seek my hurt speak of ruin,
     and meditate treachery all the day long.

13 But I am like a deaf man, I do not hear,
     like a dumb man who does not open his mouth.

14 Yea, I am like a man who does not hear,
     and in whose mouth are no rebukes.

15 But for thee, O Lord, do I wait;
     it is thou, O Lord my God, who wilt answer.

16 For I pray, "Only let them not rejoice over me,
     who boast against me when my foot slips!"

17 For I am ready to fall,
     and my pain is ever with me.

18 I confess my iniquity,
     I am sorry for my sin.

19   Those who are my foes without cause are mighty,
        and many are those who hate me wrongfully.
20   Those who render me evil for good
        are my adversaries because I follow after good.
21   Do not forsake me, O Lord!
        O my God, be not far from me!
22   Make haste to help me,
        O Lord, my salvation!

MONDAY
PREPARE YOUR HEART

† Find a quiet place where you can read and pray without distraction.

† Close your eyes and place yourself in God's presence.

† Read the following:

Reflection

It's popular today to deny the concept of sin. According to some, there are only bad choices, mistakes to move on from, and other people to blame.

Behind that dislike of calling things "sin" is outrage that God would pass judgment on me and my actions. How dare he! To that person, God is a tyrant. What a different picture we get from the Psalms.

The third Penitential Psalm, Psalm 38, begins like this: "A Psalm of David, for the memorial offering" – or, literally, "A Psalm of David, to call to mind." Far from denying the existence of sin or putting bad choices behind him, King David plunges into the mess and anguish that sin has caused in his life. He "calls it to mind" before the Lord, stares it straight in the face, and finds hope of salvation.

There are no words in Hebrew for abstract things, so this psalm is full of graphic images: arrows that have found their mark. Festering sores. Heavy burdens and traps. Friends and family who stand at a distance, enemies who laugh and provoke. These word pictures draw from me strong emotions. I can't relate to stinking sores but I know the anguish of tossing and turning in bed, thoughts churning, feeling the burden of things I've done wrong like a terrible weight. Where is the remedy?

Pray with this psalm, and you will find it.

Consider these things as you meditate on Psalm 38 during the week:

Notice the rhythm, the way David begins and ends with God, goes back and forth from bemoaning his own agony to turning to the One who can help.

Notice the progression in verses 1, 9, 15, 21-22: How does David's perspective change from one to the next?

After an examination of conscience, pour your own sorrows, your hurts and your grievances into this prayer of David. Pray along with him and find your way to his conclusion—"Make haste to help me, O Lord, my salvation!" (vs. 22)

† Pray Psalm 38 out loud, as follows.

Listen to me, O God, and show me mercy; for I am a sinner before you.
Prayerfully read the psalm.
Glory Be…

TUESDAY
READ

† Find a quiet place where you can read and pray without distraction.

† Close your eyes and place yourself in God's presence.

† Pray:

Lord, inspire me to read your Scriptures and to meditate upon them day and night.... I know that understanding and good intentions are worthless, unless rooted in your graceful love. I ask that the words of Scripture may also be not just signs on a page, but channels of grace into my heart.

—*Origen of Alexandria*

† Read Psalm 38 all the way through several times.

What stands out to you in this psalm? Are there any words or phrases that catch your eye? What do you notice about them? Record your thoughts here or in a journal if desired:

_____

_____

_____

_____

_____

_____

_____

_____

_____

_____

_____

_____

_____

_____

_____

_____

† Pray Psalm 38 out loud, as follows.

Listen to me, O God, and show me mercy; for I am a sinner before you.

Prayerfully read the psalm.

Glory Be…

TAKE IT WITH YOU

Copy the part of Psalm 38 that spoke most to you onto a small card or make a note on your smart phone. Carry it with you and meditate on it throughout the week. Repeat it until you know it by heart.

WEDNESDAY
REFLECT

† Find a quiet place where you can read and pray without distraction.

† Close your eyes and place yourself in God's presence.

† Pray:

*Lord, inspire me to read your Scriptures and to meditate upon them day
and night.... I know that understanding and good intentions are worthless,
unless rooted in your graceful love. I ask that the words of Scripture may
also be not just signs on a page, but channels of grace into my heart.*

—*Origen of Alexandria*

Reflect on Psalm 38, recalling your previous observations.

Continue to read, lingering where your heart draws you. What do
you hear God saying to you, personally? Write down what comes
to mind:

_____

_____

_____

_____

_____

_____

† Pray Psalm 38 out loud, as follows.

Listen to me, O God, and show me mercy; for I am a sinner before you.

Prayerfully read the psalm.

Glory Be…

THURSDAY
RESPOND

† Find a quiet place where you can read and pray without distraction.

† Close your eyes and place yourself in God's presence.

† Pray:

Lord, inspire me to read your Scriptures and to meditate upon them day and night.... I know that understanding and good intentions are worthless, unless rooted in your graceful love. I ask that the words of Scripture may also be not just signs on a page, but channels of grace into my heart.

—*Origen of Alexandria*

† Read Psalm 38 and recall what you have been hearing God say to your heart.

What is your response? Talk to him about it. Are you burdened by the consequences of sin in your life? Has God called to your mind a particular sin that you should take to Confession? Does the Psalm move you to gratefulness, that you should thank God? Tell him what is in your heart:

_____

_____

_____

_____

_____

---

† Pray Psalm 38 out loud, as follows.

Listen to me, O God, and show me mercy; for I am a sinner before you.

Prayerfully read the psalm.

Glory Be…

FRIDAY
REST

† Find a quiet place where you can read and pray without distraction.

† Close your eyes and place yourself in God's presence. Pray Psalm 38 out loud, as follows.

Listen to me, O God, and show me mercy; for I am a sinner before you.

Prayerfully read the psalm.

Glory Be…

Fix your gaze upon God and rest in his merciful love. Allow yourself to be quiet in his presence. Rest as though you are lying in his arms. Let him fill you with comfort and peace.

Our Father…

"Perhaps your cry will never reach the ears of men, but it is always heard by God"

—St. Augustine, Enarrationes in Psalmos, 37, 13-14

Week Four
Psalm 51 [50]

Prayer for God's mercy (Miserere)

Psalm 51

To the choirmaster. A Psalm of David, when Nathan the prophet came to him, after he had gone in to Bathsheba.

1   Have mercy on me, O God,
      according to thy steadfast love;
      according to thy abundant mercy blot out my transgressions.

2   Wash me thoroughly from my iniquity,
      and cleanse me from my sin!

3   For I know my transgressions,
      and my sin is ever before me.

4   Against thee, thee only, have I sinned,
      and done that which is evil in thy sight,
      so that thou art justified in thy sentence

and blameless in thy judgment.

5 Behold, I was brought forth in iniquity,
>   and in sin did my mother conceive me.

6 Behold, thou desirest truth in the inward being;
>   therefore teach me wisdom in my secret heart.

7 Purge me with hyssop, and I shall be clean;
>   wash me, and I shall be whiter than snow.

8 Fill me with joy and gladness;
>   let the bones which thou hast broken rejoice.

9 Hide thy face from my sins,
>   and blot out all my iniquities.

10 Create in me a clean heart, O God,
>   and put a new and right spirit within me.

11 Cast me not away from thy presence,
>   and take not thy holy Spirit from me.

12 Restore to me the joy of thy salvation,
>   and uphold me with a willing spirit.

13 Then I will teach transgressors thy ways,
>   and sinners will return to thee.

14 Deliver me from blood guiltiness, O God,
>   thou God of my salvation,
>   and my tongue will sing aloud of thy deliverance.

15 O Lord, open thou my lips,
>   and my mouth shall show forth thy praise.

16 For thou hast no delight in sacrifice;
>   were I to give a burnt offering, thou wouldst not be pleased.

17 The sacrifice acceptable to God is a broken spirit;
>   a broken and contrite heart, O God, thou wilt not despise.

18 Do good to Zion in thy good pleasure;

rebuild the walls of Jerusalem,

19 then wilt thou delight in right sacrifices,

in burnt offerings and whole burnt offerings;

then bulls will be offered on thy altar.

MONDAY
PREPARE YOUR HEART

† Find a quiet place where you can read and pray without distraction.

† Close your eyes and place yourself in God's presence.

† Read the following:

Reflection

When I was nine, I stole a big, fat, sugary Boston cream pie from the refrigerator and ate the entire thing behind the trees in the backyard.

It wasn't mine to take. We didn't have the open-frig, eat-when-you-want policy that children have today—and we never had desserts that looked like that. But even worse, I didn't know my mother chose it specially, hid it away and planned to surprise my father with it for his birthday. Not until my neighbor told on me, that is, and I watched my mother's face turn from surprise, to anger, then to pain.

It sounds like a little thing, today. But it was huge to me then. I hurt my father. Yes, I hurt my mother too, but she had meant the surprise for him. I hurt my father.

"Against thee only have I sinned," I read in Psalm 51:4, and that day comes flooding back. I couldn't get it out of my head or heart for the longest time: the shame, the disappointment, the feeling that nothing I could do could restore that surprise. "For I know my transgressions, and my sin is ever before me" (vs. 3).

There's a reason Psalm 51 is the best known of the Penitential Psalms and one of the best-loved psalms of all. It speaks to the deep pain we feel inside us when we sin, and then it shows us the mercy of God. His is the love of a Father who sees his child's stricken face – washes the tears away – and then reaches inside to create in us "a clean heart;" to breathe "a new and right spirit" within us.

Tomorrow, when you repeat Psalm 51: What words stand out to you? Here's what I see (this time, anyway):

MERCY. CLEAN.

JOY & GLADNESS.

REJOICE! RESTORE. THE JOY OF THY SALVATION.

> *"Have mercy on me, O God, according to thy steadfast love…"*
>
> *—Misereri mei, Deus.*

† Pray Psalm 51 out loud, as follows.

Listen to me, O God, and show me mercy; for I am a sinner before you.

Prayerfully read the psalm.

Glory Be…

TUESDAY
READ

† Find a quiet place where you can read and pray without distraction.

† Close your eyes and place yourself in God's presence.

† Pray:

Lord, inspire me to read your Scriptures and to meditate upon them day and night.... I know that understanding and good intentions are worthless, unless rooted in your graceful love. I ask that the words of Scripture may also be not just signs on a page, but channels of grace into my heart.

—*Origen of Alexandria*

† Read Psalm 51 all the way through several times.

What stands out to you in this psalm? Are there any words or phrases that catch your eye? What do you notice about them? Record your thoughts here or in a journal if desired:

_____

_____

_____

_____

_____

_____

_____

_____

_____

_____

_____

_____

_____

† Pray Psalm 51 out loud, as follows.

Listen to me, O God, and show me mercy; for I am a sinner before you.

Prayerfully read the psalm.

Glory Be…

TAKE IT WITH YOU

Copy the part of Psalm 51 that spoke most to you onto a small card or make a note on your smart phone. Carry it with you and meditate on it throughout the week. Repeat it until you know it by heart.

WEDNESDAY
REFLECT

† Find a quiet place where you can read and pray without distraction.

† Close your eyes and place yourself in God's presence.

† Pray:

Lord, inspire me to read your Scriptures and to meditate upon them day and night.... I know that understanding and good intentions are worthless, unless rooted in your graceful love. I ask that the words of Scripture may also be not just signs on a page, but channels of grace into my heart.

—*Origen of Alexandria*

Reflect on Psalm 51, recalling your previous observations.

Continue to read, lingering where your heart draws you. What do you hear God saying to you, personally? Write down what comes to mind:

_____

_____

_____

_____

_____

_____

† Pray Psalm 51 out loud, as follows.

Listen to me, O God, and show me mercy; for I am a sinner before you.

Prayerfully read the psalm.

Glory Be…

THURSDAY
RESPOND

† Find a quiet place where you can read and pray without distraction.

† Close your eyes and place yourself in God's presence.

† Pray:

Lord, inspire me to read your Scriptures and to meditate upon them day and night…. I know that understanding and good intentions are worthless, unless rooted in your graceful love. I ask that the words of Scripture may also be not just signs on a page, but channels of grace into my heart.

—*Origen of Alexandria*

† Read Psalm 51 and recall what you have been hearing God say to your heart.

What is your response? Talk to him about it. Are you burdened by the consequences of sin in your life? Has God called to your mind a particular sin that you should take to Confession? Does the Psalm move you to gratefulness, that you should thank God? Tell him what is in your heart:

† Pray Psalm 51 out loud, as follows.

Listen to me, O God, and show me mercy; for I am a sinner before you.

Prayerfully read the psalm.

Glory Be…

 FRIDAY
REST

† Find a quiet place where you can read and pray without distraction.

† Close your eyes and place yourself in God's presence. Pray Psalm 51 out loud, as follows.

Listen to me, O God, and show me mercy; for I am a sinner before you.

Prayerfully read the psalm.

Glory Be…

Fix your gaze upon God and rest in his merciful love. Allow yourself to be quiet in his presence. Rest as though you are lying in his arms. Let him fill you with comfort and peace.

Our Father…

O give thanks to the Lord, for he is good,
for his steadfast love endures for ever.

—Psalm 136:1

Week Five
Psalm 102 [101]

Prayer in distress and affliction

Psalm 102

A prayer of one afflicted, when he is faint and pours out his complaint before the Lord.

1   Hear my prayer, O Lord;
>   let my cry come to thee!
2   Do not hide thy face from me
>   in the day of my distress!
>   Incline thy ear to me;
>   answer me speedily in the day when I call!
3   For my days pass away like smoke,
>   and my bones burn like a furnace.
4   My heart is smitten like grass, and withered;
>   I forget to eat my bread.

5   Because of my loud groaning
        my bones cleave to my flesh.

6   I am like a vulture of the wilderness,
        like an owl of the waste places;

7   I lie awake,
        I am like a lonely bird on the housetop.

8   All the day my enemies taunt me,
        those who deride me use my name for a curse.

9   For I eat ashes like bread,
        and mingle tears with my drink,

10 because of thy indignation and anger;
        for thou hast taken me up and thrown me away.

11 My days are like an evening shadow;
        I wither away like grass.

12 But thou, O Lord, art enthroned for ever;
        thy name endures to all generations.

13 Thou wilt arise and have pity on Zion;
        it is the time to favor her;
        the appointed time has come.

14 For thy servants hold her stones dear,
        and have pity on her dust.

15 The nations will fear the name of the Lord,
        and all the kings of the earth thy glory.

16 For the Lord will build up Zion,
        he will appear in his glory;

17 he will regard the prayer of the destitute,
        and will not despise their supplication.

18 Let this be recorded for a generation to come,
        so that a people yet unborn may praise the Lord:

19 that he looked down from his holy height,
>   from heaven the Lord looked at the earth,

20 to hear the groans of the prisoners,
>   to set free those who were doomed to die;

21 that men may declare in Zion the name of the Lord,
>   and in Jerusalem his praise,

22 when peoples gather together,
>   and kingdoms, to worship the Lord.

23 He has broken my strength in mid-course;
>   he has shortened my days.

24 "O my God," I say, "take me not hence
>   in the midst of my days,
>   thou whose years endure
>   throughout all generations!"

25 Of old thou didst lay the foundation of the earth,
>   and the heavens are the work of thy hands.

26 They will perish, but thou dost endure;
>   they will all wear out like a garment.
>   Thou changest them like raiment, and they pass away;

27 but thou art the same, and thy years have no end.

28 The children of thy servants shall dwell secure;
>   their posterity shall be established before thee.

MONDAY
PREPARE YOUR HEART

† Find a quiet place where you can read and pray without distraction.

† Close your eyes and place yourself in God's presence.

† Read the following:

Reflection

The beginning of the end of my Grandmother's life came early one morning. I knew she had cancer; but to my young and hopeful mind she would survive. What signaled the change I do not know, but I woke to hushed whispers and frantic activity. A blood cot to the brain, they said.

I loved my Grandma. She was a towering presence of love and solid faith, a careful listener, a font of wise advice. The realization that her life was nearly over hit me like a wall. As the others left in the ambulance, I turned the water as hot as it would go, drowned my pain in the shower and screamed at God.

I feel the intensity of that prayer in Psalm 102, the fifth Penitential Psalm.

I feel its audacity, too: me telling God what he can and can't do. Demanding his assistance. Presuming his attention and immediate help. The opening plea contains five strong imperatives, each one intensely directed at God: "Hear my prayer." "Let my cry come to thee!" "Do not hide." "Incline thy ear." "Answer me speedily!" This may be a desperate cry but already there is hope: it is addressed to someone the psalmist has a claim on. God may not "owe" him anything, but there is nothing so strong as the claim of love.

Because of God's immense love for us we can throw ourselves on him in our pain, whatever its source, even in the self-inflicted pain of sin. We can cry, we can yell, we can beg like a child who screams "Mo….m!" at the first sign of trouble, who assumes she can and will help. God can and will help, and he wants to.

When you read Psalm 102 this week, try to listen with your ears. Read it out loud, if that helps. Pay attention when you read "But thou…" in vs. 12. "But God" has been a great turning point in my life, a reminder that whatever else is true, "But God" – there is a greater reality.

What makes the difference to the psalmist, after that "But"? Look for indications of God's character and promises. Things he will do because of those. Things he has done that prove he is able. Take your own prayer of confession before him, and rest in the psalmist's final realization: "but thou art the same, and thy years have no end." The psalmist's God is your God, too.

Note: It seems that over the course of the years, a plea on behalf of the people of Israel was inserted into the plea of this individual (see vss. 13-22). Possibly the original prayer was felt to be particularly apt, to those who returned home to Jerusalem after exile in Babylon. If you can't pray the first part with meaning for yourself today, maybe you can pray the entire Psalm on behalf of God's church.+ + +

   † Pray Psalm 102 out loud, as follows.
      Listen to me, O God, and show me mercy; for I am a sinner before you.
      Prayerfully read the psalm.
      Glory Be…

TUESDAY
READ

† Find a quiet place where you can read and pray without distraction.

† Close your eyes and place yourself in God's presence.

† Pray:

Lord, inspire me to read your Scriptures and to meditate upon them day and night.... I know that understanding and good intentions are worthless, unless rooted in your graceful love. I ask that the words of Scripture may also be not just signs on a page, but channels of grace into my heart.

—*Origen of Alexandria*

† Read Psalm 102 all the way through several times.

What stands out to you in this psalm? Are there any words or phrases that catch your eye? What do you notice about them? Record your thoughts here or in a journal if desired:

_____

_____

_____

_____

_____

_____

_____

....

....

....

....

....

....

....

....

....

....

....

....

....

† Pray Psalm 102 out loud, as follows.

Listen to me, O God, and show me mercy; for I am a sinner before you.

Prayerfully read the psalm.

Glory Be…

TAKE IT WITH YOU

Copy the part of Psalm 102 that spoke most to you onto a small card or make a note on your smart phone. Carry it with you and meditate on it throughout the week. Repeat it until you know it by heart.

WEDNESDAY
REFLECT

† Find a quiet place where you can read and pray without distraction.

† Close your eyes and place yourself in God's presence.

† Pray:

Lord, inspire me to read your Scriptures and to meditate upon them day and night.... I know that understanding and good intentions are worthless, unless rooted in your graceful love. I ask that the words of Scripture may also be not just signs on a page, but channels of grace into my heart.

—Origen of Alexandria

Reflect on Psalm 102, recalling your previous observations. Continue to read, lingering where your heart draws you. What do you hear God saying to you, personally? Write down what comes to mind:

_____

_____

_____

_____

_____

_____

_____

---

† Pray Psalm 102 out loud, as follows.

Listen to me, O God, and show me mercy; for I am a sinner before you.

Prayerfully read the psalm.

Glory Be…

THURSDAY

RESPOND

† Find a quiet place where you can read and pray without distraction.

† Close your eyes and place yourself in God's presence.

† Pray:

Lord, inspire me to read your Scriptures and to meditate upon them day and night…. I know that understanding and good intentions are worthless, unless rooted in your graceful love. I ask that the words of Scripture may also be not just signs on a page, but channels of grace into my heart.

—*Origen of Alexandria*

† Read Psalm 102 and recall what you have been hearing God say to your heart.

What is your response? Talk to him about it. Are you burdened by the consequences of sin in your life? Has God called to your mind a particular sin that you should take to Confession? Does the Psalm move you to gratefulness, that you should thank God? Tell him what is in your heart:

---

† Pray Psalm 102 out loud, as follows.

Listen to me, O God, and show me mercy; for I am a sinner before you.

Prayerfully read the psalm.

Glory Be…

FRIDAY
REST

† Find a quiet place where you can read and pray without distraction.

† Close your eyes and place yourself in God's presence. Pray
Psalm 102 out loud, as follows.

Listen to me, O God, and show me mercy; for I am a sinner before you.

Prayerfully read the psalm.

Glory Be…

Fix your gaze upon God and rest in his merciful love.
Allow yourself to be quiet in his presence. Rest as though you are
lying in his arms. Let him fill you with comfort *and peace.*

Our Father…

I will heal their faithlessness;
I will love them freely,

—Hosea 14:4

Week Six
Psalm 130 [129]

Prayer from the depths; a soul waiting for God
(De Profundis)

Psalm 130

A Song of Ascents.

1   Out of the depths I cry to thee, O Lord!

2   Lord, hear my voice!

       Let thy ears be attentive

       to the voice of my supplications!

3   If thou, O Lord, shouldst mark iniquities,

       Lord, who could stand?

4   But there is forgiveness with thee,

       that thou mayest be feared.

5   I wait for the Lord, my soul waits,

       and in his word I hope;

6   my soul waits for the Lord

   more than watchmen for the morning,

   more than watchmen for the morning.

7   O Israel, hope in the Lord!

   For with the Lord there is steadfast love,

   and with him is plenteous redemption.

8   And he will redeem Israel

   from all his iniquities.

MONDAY
PREPARE YOUR HEART

† Find a quiet place where you can read and pray without distraction.

† Close your eyes and place yourself in God's presence.

† Read the following:

Reflection

One of my enduring memories of 9/11 is the packed church that night. Nobody was told to come, there was no Mass, no scheduled prayer service – the people just came. We came together in our grief, our fear, our incomprehension. We huddled in silent prayer and wept. Instinctively, we knew that God was there and that he would hear us.

"Out of the depths I cry to thee, O Lord! Lord, hear my voice!"

Sin can cast us into the depths as surely as tragedy can. Think of Jonah, running from God as most of us have done at one time or another. Running as far as he can, then being cast into the sea: "the waters closed in over me, the deep was round about me; weeds were wrapped about my head…" (Jon 2:5). Sin chokes and entangles us, weighs us down, takes us far from God.

And yet – neither the sea nor the body of the fish could keep Jonah's cry from reaching the ears of God.

"Out of the depths I cry to thee, O Lord! Lord, hear my voice!"

Psalm 130, the sixth of our Penitential Psalms, celebrates the open "ear" of God. When you read it, notice the shout of confident hope at the end! Because of God's steadfast love, no sin can put us beyond his reach (except the sin of refusing his grace, for he will not force redemption on us).

Notice all the times these eight short verses mention watching or waiting. They culminate in a beautiful image of a soul that waits for the Lord "more than watchmen for the morning." Anyone who has camped outside and woken in the wee hours can relate to the solitary man on the city wall: alone with his thoughts and his fears, eyes straining against the dark, yearning for those first rays of light that will send him to his bed.

This image highlights the intensity of the psalmist's yearning – but it also shows the certainty of hope. The morning will come, his waiting will not be in vain. And God's "plenteous redemption" (vs. 7) will come. The light of his forgiveness can pierce any pit we hide in.

All we have to do is call to him.

† Pray Psalm 130 out loud, as follows.
Listen to me, O God, and show me mercy; for I am a sinner before you.
Prayerfully read the psalm.
Glory Be…

TUESDAY
READ

† Find a quiet place where you can read and pray without distraction.

† Close your eyes and place yourself in God's presence.

† Pray:

Lord, inspire me to read your Scriptures and to meditate upon them day and night.... I know that understanding and good intentions are worthless, unless rooted in your graceful love. I ask that the words of Scripture may also be not just signs on a page, but channels of grace into my heart.

—Origen of Alexandria

† Read Psalm 130 all the way through several times.

What stands out to you in this psalm? Are there any words or phrases that catch your eye? What do you notice about them? Record your thoughts here or in a journal if desired:

---

† Pray Psalm 130 out loud, as follows.

Listen to me, O God, and show me mercy; for I am a sinner before you.

Prayerfully read the psalm.

Glory Be…

TAKE IT WITH YOU

Copy the part of Psalm 130 that spoke most to you onto a small card or make a note on your smart phone. Carry it with you and meditate on it throughout the week. Repeat it until you know it by heart.

WEDNESDAY
REFLECT

† Find a quiet place where you can read and pray without distraction.

† Close your eyes and place yourself in God's presence.

† Pray:

Lord, inspire me to read your Scriptures and to meditate upon them day and night.... I know that understanding and good intentions are worthless, unless rooted in your graceful love. I ask that the words of Scripture may also be not just signs on a page, but channels of grace into my heart.

—Origen of Alexandria

Reflect on Psalm 130, recalling your previous observations. Continue to read, lingering where your heart draws you. What do you hear God saying to you, personally? Write down what comes to mind:

_____

_____

_____

_____

_____

_____

_____

---

† Pray Psalm 130 out loud, as follows.

Listen to me, O God, and show me mercy; for I am a sinner before you.

Prayerfully read the psalm.

Glory Be…

THURSDAY
RESPOND

† Find a quiet place where you can read and pray without distraction.

† Close your eyes and place yourself in God's presence.

† Pray:

Lord, inspire me to read your Scriptures and to meditate upon them day and night…. I know that understanding and good intentions are worthless, unless rooted in your graceful love. I ask that the words of Scripture may also be not just signs on a page, but channels of grace into my heart.

—*Origen of Alexandria*

† Read Psalm 130 and recall what you have been hearing God say to your heart.

What is your response? Talk to him about it. Are you burdened by the consequences of sin in your life? Has God called to your mind a particular sin that you should take to Confession? Does the Psalm move you to gratefulness, that you should thank God? Tell him what is in your heart:

† Pray Psalm 130 out loud, as follows.

Listen to me, O God, and show me mercy; for I am a sinner before you.

Prayerfully read the psalm.

Glory Be…

FRIDAY
REST

† Find a quiet place where you can read and pray without distraction.

† Close your eyes and place yourself in God's presence. Pray Psalm 130 out loud, as follows.

Listen to me, O God, and show me mercy; for I am a sinner before you.

Prayerfully read the psalm.

Glory Be…

 Fix your gaze upon God and rest in his merciful love. Allow yourself to be quiet in his presence. Rest as though you are lying in his arms. Let him fill you with comfort and peace.

Our Father…

…hope in the Lord!
For with the Lord there is steadfast love,
and with him is plenteous redemption.

—Psalm 130:7

Holy Week:
Psalm 143 [142]

Prayer of supplication, for deliverance

Psalm 143

A Psalm of David.

1   Hear my prayer, O Lord;
      give ear to my supplications!
      In thy faithfulness answer me, in thy righteousness!

2   Enter not into judgment with thy servant;
      for no man living is righteous before thee.

3   For the enemy has pursued me;
      he has crushed my life to the ground;
      he has made me sit in darkness like those long dead.

4   Therefore my spirit faints within me;
      my heart within me is appalled.

5   I remember the days of old,

I meditate on all that thou hast done;

I muse on what thy hands have wrought.

6 I stretch out my hands to thee;

my soul thirsts for thee like a parched land. [Selah]

7 Make haste to answer me, O Lord!

My spirit fails!

Hide not thy face from me,

lest I be like those who go down to the Pit.

8 Let me hear in the morning of thy steadfast love,

for in thee I put my trust.

Teach me the way I should go,

for to thee I lift up my soul.

9 Deliver me, O Lord, from my enemies!

I have fled to thee for refuge!

10 Teach me to do thy will,

for thou art my God!

Let thy good spirit lead me

on a level path!

11 For thy name's sake, O Lord, preserve my life!

In thy righteousness bring me out of trouble!

12 And in thy steadfast love cut off my enemies,

and destroy all my adversaries,

for I am thy servant.

MONDAY
PREPARE YOUR HEART

† Find a quiet place where you can read and pray without distraction.

† Close your eyes and place yourself in God's presence.

† Read the following:

Reflection

The final Penitential Psalm, Psalm 143, takes us to the foot of the cross on Good Friday.

The psalmist has reached the end of his rope. His "spirit faints," his heart is "appalled" (vs. 4). He feels trapped and abandoned even by God, on the verge of death.

Sitting in darkness, crushed to the ground, the psalmist turns to the Lord. My own temptation when I am overwhelmed is to wallow in depression and doubt, to sink further into the pit. That's why I love praying the psalms. Meditating on the first verses, I really relate. I enter into the suffering, sink low in my soul. Then verses 5-6 snap me out of it. They give me a recipe for a changed heart:

> **I remember** *the days of old*
> **I meditate** *on all that thou hast done;*
> **I muse** *on what thy hands have wrought.*
> **I stretch out** *my hands to thee;*
> **My soul thirsts** *for thee like a parched land.*

Do you see how the attention of the psalmist moves? From being crushed in darkness, eyes on the ground and the pit – to recalling

God's past goodness and faithfulness – to meditating on those things – at last to stretching upward, every fiber of his being seeking help from the Lord. Instead of drinking the dust, his mouth is now open to the source of living water.

Remember. Meditate. Muse. Stretch out. Thirst.

Today, thinking of that first Good Friday:

> **I remember** what God did to solve our problems. He took our sins, our pain, our suffering on himself.

> **I meditate** on what that meant. When the wave of death rolled in, he bowed his head, dove under it.

> **I muse** on the result. He allowed it to crush him – then rose triumphant on the other side.

> **I choose to stretch out.** To lift my eyes from my sins and troubles and put them on God. I remember what he has done and stretch my hands up toward the cross.

> **I thirst** for you, O God! As your Son thirsted on the cross.

> In your death, deliver me O Lord. Take my pains, my sins, and let me rise with you to life!

Without a death – there can be no resurrection.

> † Pray Psalm 143 out loud, as follows.
> *Listen to me, O God, and show me mercy; for I am a sinner before you.*
> Prayerfully read the psalm.
> *Glory Be…*

✧ TUESDAY ✧
READ

† Find a quiet place where you can read and pray without distraction.

† Close your eyes and place yourself in God's presence.

† Pray:

Lord, inspire me to read your Scriptures and to meditate upon them day and night.... I know that understanding and good intentions are worthless, unless rooted in your graceful love. I ask that the words of Scripture may also be not just signs on a page, but channels of grace into my heart.

—*Origen of Alexandria*

† Read Psalm 143 all the way through several times.

✎ **What stands out to you in this psalm?** Are there any words or phrases that catch your eye? What do you notice about them? Record your thoughts here or in a journal if desired:

_____

_____

_____

_____

_____

_____

_____

_____

_____

_____

_____

_____

_____

_____

_____

_____

_____

_____

_____

† Pray Psalm 143 out loud, as follows.

Listen to me, O God, and show me mercy; for I am a sinner before you.

Prayerfully read the psalm.

Glory Be…

TAKE IT WITH YOU

Copy the part of Psalm 143 that spoke most to you onto a small card or make a note on your smart phone. Carry it with you and meditate on it throughout the week. Repeat it until you know it by heart.

Ꮖ WEDNESDAY Ꮖ
REFLECT

† Find a quiet place where you can read and pray without distraction.

† Close your eyes and place yourself in God's presence.

† Pray:

*Lord, inspire me to read your Scriptures and to meditate upon them day
and night.... I know that understanding and good intentions are worthless,
unless rooted in your graceful love. I ask that the words of Scripture may
also be not just signs on a page, but channels of grace into my heart.*

——Origen of Alexandria

Reflect on Psalm 143, recalling your previous observations.
Continue to read, lingering where your heart draws you. What do
you hear God saying to you, personally? Write down what comes
to mind:

† Pray Psalm 143 out loud, as follows.

Listen to me, O God, and show me mercy; for I am a sinner before you.

Prayerfully read the psalm.

Glory Be…

THURSDAY
RESPOND

† Find a quiet place where you can read and pray without distraction.

† Close your eyes and place yourself in God's presence.

† Pray:

Lord, inspire me to read your Scriptures and to meditate upon them day and night.... I know that understanding and good intentions are worthless, unless rooted in your graceful love. I ask that the words of Scripture may also be not just signs on a page, but channels of grace into my heart.

—*Origen of Alexandria*

† Read Psalm 143 and recall what you have been hearing God say to your heart.

What is your response? Talk to him about it. Are you burdened by the consequences of sin in your life? Has God called to your mind a particular sin that you should take to Confession? Does the Psalm move you to gratefulness, that you should thank God? Tell him what is in your heart:

† Pray Psalm 143 out loud, as follows.

Listen to me, O God, and show me mercy; for I am a sinner before you.

Prayerfully read the psalm.

Glory Be…

FRIDAY
REST

† Find a quiet place where you can read and pray without distraction.

† Close your eyes and place yourself in God's presence. Pray
Psalm 143 out loud, as follows.

Listen to me, O God, and show me mercy; for I am a sinner before you.
Prayerfully read the psalm.

Glory Be…

Fix your gaze upon God and rest in his merciful love.
Allow yourself to be quiet in his presence. Rest as though you are
lying in his arms. Let him fill you with comfort and peace.

Our Father…

He was wounded for our transgressions,
he was bruised for our iniquities;
upon him was the chastisement that made us whole,
and with his stripes we are healed.

—Isaiah 53:5

Now that Lent is over...
What now?

"Exercise your mind, feed it daily with Holy Scripture"

—*St. Jerome*

I hope you've been blessed by your daily journey through the Penitential Psalms! As we head back into Ordinary Time, consider setting aside a few minutes each day to re-connect with God in his Word. He's sure to bless you!

Here are seven ideas to get you started:

1. **Grab a lectionary** and read the Gospel every day for a year (don't wait to go to Mass).

2. **Read a Psalm a day.** When you're done, go back to your favorites. Or get familiar with praying the Liturgy of the Hours.

3. **Start with Acts or Paul's letters** and make your way through the New Testament. Take your time, even if it's just a few sentences a day. Let it soak in. Listen and pray to find the Word in his words.

4. I once spent an entire school year reading **a chapter of Proverbs a day**. There are 31 chapters, so it's easy to go to the day you're on.

5. **Don't be afraid** to read something good over and over. You might even memorize a book that way, without trying. Think what God could do in your soul if his Word begins to be part of you....

6. Spend the summer making your way through **the 90-day *Bible Timeline* reading plan** from The Great Adventure Catholic Bible Study Program. It'll take you through the entire biblical narrative (fourteen books in all) in three months. Sign up at http://bit.ly/1Nj6oY5 to have a free daily message, reading assignment, and question from me sent to your inbox. When you're done, go back and take your time praying through your favorite parts.

7. **Read through those same readings in a year** instead of over three months by reading just one chapter a day.

Download a checklist at http://bit.ly/1QcATn1 or read with the help of the *Bible Timeline Guided Journal*, available from Ascension Press.

Let me know what you plan and how you get on with it! You can email me at sarah@comeintotheword.com. And may the Lord richly bless you as you read.

Visit www.ComeIntotheWord.com for weekly reflections
on the Bible and the Catholic faith and helpful
information on reading and studying the Bible.

Sarah Christmyer is co-developer and founding editor of *The Great Adventure* Catholic Bible study program. The author of numerous Bible studies, she speaks at conferences and retreats on topics related to Scripture and the Catholic faith. Sarah is an adjunct faculty member at St. Charles Borromeo Seminary, Philadelphia. She blogs at her website — www.ComeIntotheWord.com — and at www.BibleStudyforCatholics.com and www.CatholicVineyard.com.

.

Made in the USA
Middletown, DE
03 March 2019